The animals and the weather were different a long time ago. The First Peoples of Australia saw many big animals. The weather was colder than today. It was called the Ice Age when the First People came to Australia.

People first came to the north of Australia. They came across the sea in small boats. The weather was warm in the north. Inland it became very dry and cold.

Australia had rivers going inland. Canoes were used to collect river plants and hunt for food. The rivers had fish, turtles, birds, eels and plant foods.

Rainforests had many fruits, seeds, and animals. These forests were very warm with many trees. A lot of rain fell on the forest. The forest is very wet. Shelters had to stop the rain.

On the coast people could find plenty of food and shelter. Fish and turtles in the sea were hunted. A large lizard could be very dangerous.

In forests and swamps big animals could eat the grasses and reeds. The forests were close to the rivers. There were many animals to hunt for food.

People lived along the coast of Australia. Fishing could be done from canoes. As the people went south it got colder.

Along the coastal areas there were trees growing in the water. These trees were called mangroves. Mangroves hold the soil and mud together. Little fish and crabs live among the mangroves.

In the dry and cold areas there were large plains. The people could hunt large animals and birds. Life would have been hard as it was very cold.

In the mountains it was very cold. Animals need long fur to stay warm. The First Peoples went hunting in these areas. It was a very cold place with not a lot of food.

Forests were along the mountains. Animals could be hunted in these forests. Kangaroos lived in these areas.

The mountains were covered in snow all year. The First Peoples would have found it very cold in these mountains.